JOKE & RIDDLE BONANZA

MICHAEL J. PELLOWSKI

Illustrated by Sanford Hoffman

STERLING CHILDREN'S BOOKS
New York

STERLING CHILDREN'S BOOKS
New York

An Imprint of Sterling Publishing
387 Park Avenue South
New York, NY 10016

To Morgan J. Pellowski, author of "Petty Theft,"
and my beloved son, who is sorely missed.

STERLING CHILDREN'S BOOKS and the distinctive Sterling Children's
Books logo are trademarks of Sterling Publishing Co., Inc.

ISBN 978-1-4027-8837-6

Distributed in Canada by Sterling Publishing
^{c}/o Canadian Manda Group, 165 Dufferin Street
Toronto, Ontario, Canada M6K 3H6
Distributed in the United Kingdom by GMC Distribution Services
Castle Place, 166 High Street, Lewes, East Sussex, England BN7 1XU
Distributed in Australia by Capricorn Link (Australia) Pty. Ltd.
P.O. Box 704, Windsor, NSW 2756, Australia

For information about custom editions, special sales, and premium and
corporate purchases, please contact Sterling Special Sales at 800-805-5489
or specialsales@sterlingpublishing.com.

Manufactured in the United States of America
Lot #:
2   4   6   8   10   9   7   5   3   1
11/11

www.sterlingpublishing.com/kids

CONTENTS

1.
FRIGHT-FULLY FUNNY

What giant buzzing insects lived long ago?
Beehistoric monsters.

What does a Brontosaurus have on the ends of its feet?
Brontoes!

Which dinosaur is a body builder?
Tyrannosaurus Flex.

What monster lives in the mountains and alters men's suits?

The Abominable Sewman.

When does a monster duck wake up?

At the quack of doom.

What do female monsters discuss when they're alone together?

Ghoul talk.

What's noisy and performs at parades in space?

A Martian (marching) band.

What peculiar guy is in charge of the Starship Enterprise?

Captain Quirk.

SILLY SPACE BOOKS

How to Build Robots
by Ann Droid

Successful Rocket Launches
by Count M. Down

Living in Space
by Otto Griswald (this world)

Heavenly Bodies
by Lotta Stars

Space Weapons
by Ray Gunn

What is woolly and from outer space?
A Ewe-F-O.

THE TOMBSTONE OF R2D2:

What do you call a cartoon character from the moon?

A luna toon.

What would you get if you crossed a yellow mummy and a green mummy?

A golden mouldy.

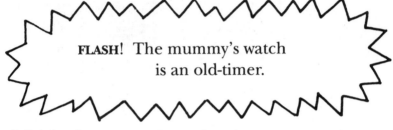

FLASH! The mummy's watch is an old-timer.

Which ghost came from the planet Krypton?

Spookerman.

What do trendy ghosts wear?

Designer boo jeans.

Which monster makes designer jeans?

Calvin Frankenklein.

Where does Calvin Frankenklein live?

In Pantsylvania.

Where do monster TV shows go when they're taken off the air?

To Cancelvania.

What did the girl say to the Invisible Man?

"I can't see you anymore."

What monster lives in a clothes dryer?
Kling Kong.

What would you get if you crossed King Kong with shoe polish?
The biggest monkey shine in the world.

What would you get if you crossed the Wolfman with King Kong?
A very hairy ape.

What would you get if you crossed the Wolfman with a pack of dogs?
A werewoof-woof-woof.

IGOR: Knock-Knock.
   IVAN: Who's there?
IGOR: Werewolves.
   IVAN: Werewolves who?
IGOR: Werewolves are—you won't find me.

What animated ghost movie was nominated for an
Academy Award?
"Boo-ty and the Beast."

Why did Mr. and Mrs. Zombie split up?
Their marriage was only until death do they part.

What is the one thing a zombie never needs to
buy?
Life insurance.

Where do zombies live?
On dead-end streets.

What is a zombie's favorite TV comedy show?
"Saturday Night Dead."

Where did the zombie finish in the Transylvania Marathon race?
Dead last!

Who is spooky and checks new haunted houses for problems?
The Building Inspectre.

WHAT'S IN A HAUNTED HOUSE?

Alarmed clocks

Frightful decorations

Mon-stairs

Window shudders (shutters)

Batrooms

Bed glooms

Scream doors

When do ghosts go out haunting?
Whenever the spirit moves them.

What kind of rugs do you find in a haunted house?
No rugs—wail-to-wail carpeting.

WACKY ROBOTS

THE OWL ROBOT—also known as WHO-R-U

THE CAT ROBOT—also known as KIT-10

THE RAPPER ROBOT—also known as
    I.M.2-COOL

THE HEALTH FOOD ROBOT—also known as
    GOOD-4-U

Show me a man who has a metal robot named
William . . . and I'll show you a guy with an iron
will.

EARTHMAN: Do you recognize the word Saturn?
MARTIAN: It has a familiar ring to it.

DAFFYNITION
ASTRONUT—**Acorn from space.**

What did Mr. Spaceman grow in his garden?
  Alien beans (beings).

What aliens like to carve figures out of wood?
The whittle men from Mars.

Why did the alien lawyers go to court?
To settle a space suit.

MR. SATURN: I'm leaving now.
MS. VENUS: Give me a ring later.

What is the favorite game of monster musicians?
"Maim That Tune."

What is a zombie's favorite rock group?
The Grateful Dead.

What would you get if you crossed a Japanese
monster with Fort Knox?
Godzillions.

MAD SCIENTIST: I crossed a witch doctor with a bakery.

GHOUL: What did you get?

MAD SCIENTIST: Voodough.

What happened to the voodoo doll at the restaurant?

It got stuck with the check.

Where does Dracula never go for dinner?

To a stakehouse.

What disease do grave-diggers sometimes get?

Bury-Bury.

Why do Egyptian undertakers make good detectives?

They're good at wrapping up their cases.

FAMOUS GHOSTS FROM LONG AGO

Daniel Boo-one

Balboo-a

Pochahauntus

Where does a lady ghost sleep?
In her boo-doir.

FRANKENSTEIN: How did you win that Varsity letter?
SASQUATCH: Don't you know I'm a big track star?

Why did the monster try out for the Olympics?
She wanted to win a ghoul medal.

What gum do ghost
snakes chew?
Wiggley Spirit gum.

How do you make a zombie car?
With a dead battery.

What do haunted chickens lay?
Devilled eggs.

HOW'S YOUR CREEPY JOB?

"I can't see myself working here much longer."—The Invisible Man

"I'm just moonlighting."—The Wolfman

How does a ghostbuster stay in shape?
He rides an exorcise bike!

IGOR: Why is that monster carrying a broom?
IVAN: He's the Grim Sweeper.

What do you get if you cross an owl with an alien weapon?
A Whoo-Ray Gun.

FRIGHTFUL FLASH!
Rodan is a birdbrain.

2.
GIGGLE GRABBAG

What's gray, weighs five tons, and bounces?
An elephant making a bungee jump.

What does the sky do when it gets dirty?
It showers.

Which pirate made a lot of mistakes?
Wrong John Silver.

What's brown, lumpy, and goes "choo choo"?
A gravy train.

What did the kiln say to the clay pot?
"I thought I fired you already."

POLICE CHIEF: Did you follow the crooks across the
    frozen lake?
COP: Yes, Chief, but they gave me the slip.

Mother Nature, you're headed for a Fall!

SIGN IN A NURSERY

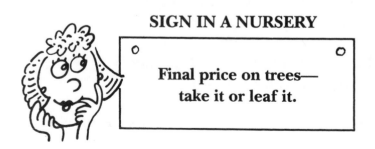

**Final price on trees—
take it or leaf it.**

AN INSULTING FAREWELL

To a Mapmaker . . . Get lost!

To an Airplane Pilot . . . Take off!

To a Transferred Worker . . . Get moving!

To a "B" Student . . . Buzz off!

To a Garbage Man . . . Haul it out of here!

To a Navy Frogman . . . Go jump in the lake!

To an Acrobat . . . Go take a flying leap!

To a Rock Musician . . . Beat it!

Mack: How can you keep a nervous horse from running out of the barn?
Zack: Stall him.

What would you get if you crossed a lariat and a magician?
Rope tricks.

Jack: I can make you giggle any time I want to.
Mack: Ha! That's a laugh!

TIME-OUTS

MR. CLOCK: Can I have a minute of your time?
MRS. CLOCK: I'm not tocking to you.

WAITER: What will you have, Mr. Clock?
MR. CLOCK: A minute steak.

PSYCHOLOGIST: You are not a wristwatch.
PATIENT: I want a second opinion.

What do you say when you bounce a clock on a trampoline?
"Time's up!"

What did Mrs. Watch say to her shy son?
"Take your hands off your face."

What did Nanny Wristwatch say to the impatient doorknob?
"Wait your turn. I only have two hands."

What ticks and plays music?
A watchband.

Why did the silly kid tattoo alarm clocks on his palms?
He wanted to have time on his hands.

How do sheep keep their feet warm?
They wear wool socks.

How did the sheep get into trouble?
She fell in with a baa crowd.

What goes "buzz-buzz," has a hard shell, and gets served on an airplane?
A roasted bee nut.

What would you get if you crossed clothing static with Elvis Presley?
The Kling of Rock and Roll.

What comedian works at the bank?
The joke teller.

What do you call four dirty pigs who sing together?
A barber slop quartet.

What would you get if you crossed bank checks
with skunks?
Money odors (orders).

What would you get if you crossed an igloo with a
tent?
An ice teepee.

Why did King Arthur buy long woollen
underwear?
For cold winter knights.

THEY'RE A PERFECT MATCH

She's cold-hearted . . . and he has ice water in his veins.

She wears a ponytail . . . and he likes to horse around.

She has a dirty mind . . . and he has a filthy mouth.

She's a real dog . . . and he's a real animal.

She's a bad cook . . . and he has no taste.

TED: Why did the Beetles break up?
NED: They started to bug each other.

BEACH BALL: I'm going to a beach party.
GOLF BALL: Big deal! I'm going to a tee party.

How do you mail a letter to a fence?
Use the fence post.

TILLIE: A penny for your thoughts?
MILLIE: That makes cents to me.

Where do lumberjacks buy axes?
At a chopping mall.

Why did the margarine buy a rabbit's foot?
It wanted to have butter luck.

FUNNY BUNNIES

What do you get if you cross a banana
peel with an accident-prone bunny?
A falling hare.

What organization did Mr. Rabbit join?
The Hare Club for Men.

What do you get if you cross a baby chick
with a baby bunny?
Peeper Cottontail.

What should you say when a rabbit sits on
an ant hill?
"Look out for bugs, Bunny!"

Why was the donkey at the police station?
The cops were trying to pin something on it.

MR. DUCK: Wow! Did you hear the great voice on that young hen?'
MR. ROOSTER: Ah, it was just beginner's cluck.

Why was the stork coughing?
He had a frog in his throat.

Where do travelling cows disappear mysteriously?
In the Ber-mooo-da Triangle.

What do you call a rooster with a bad sunburn?
A fried chicken.

FARMER: My sheep won the million dollar lottery.
MAN: Lucky ewe!

3.
FURNISHED
RUMORS

Where should you put a dirty cow?
In a shower stall.

Show me George Washington's kitchen . . .
and I'll show you a presidential cabinet.

Why did the kitchen cabinet go to the
psychologist?
Because it kept talking to its shelf.

Which piece of furniture plays football?
The end table.

KING ARTHUR: How much do your rooms cost?
INNKEEPER: Twenty dollars per knight.

HUSBAND: I can't decide if we should buy a new bed or not.
WIFE: Me neither. Let's sleep on it.

HOUSE: Ouch! Ouch! Ouch!
CARPENTER: What's wrong with you?
HOUSE: Just window panes.

SIGN ON A SNOW PLOW COMPANY

Let us break the ice
for you.

What would you get if you crossed a baseball pitcher with carpeting?
Throw rugs.

What would you get if you crossed a foam cushion with an egg?
A padded shell.

HUSBAND: I bought a light bulb that had a four-leaf clover in it.
WIFE: Watt luck!

Where do large black birds keep their suits?
In a crow's (clothes) closet.

Which piece of furniture pouts a lot?
The whining room table.

What would you get if you crossed a werewolf with a piece of furniture?
A hairy chest.

Why did the dresser turn red?
Its drawers fell down.

What did the dining room table say at its meeting with the kitchen table?
"Let's find someone to chair our committee."

How did the TVs celebrate after cable was installed?
They held a great reception.

Why did Mrs. Crow have a big phone bill?
She made too many long distance caws.

What did the farmer plant in his sofa?
Couch potatoes.

4.
LIBRARY LAUGHS

MATT: Did you read *Moby Dick*?
PAT: Yes. It was a whale of a tale!

MATT: Did you read *Gone With the Wind*?
PAT: Yes. It blew me away.

MATT: How did you like "Dr. Jekyll and Mr. Hyde"?
PAT: It was good and bad.

AL: What is the opposite of a tall tale?
CAL: A short story.

What do comedians read?
Comic books.

What do musicians read?
Notebooks.

What do burglars read?
Crook books.

What do skunks read?
Best-smellers.

What do cowboys from Dallas read?
Tex books.

MAN: Do you have any books on gambling?
LIBRARIAN: You bet!

MILLIE: How was that book on chronic illnesses?
TILLIE: Sickening.

LOONY LIBRARY BOOKS

Who Needs a Job?
by I. Quitt

Visit Las Vegas
by Hy Roller

How to Insult People
by U.R.A. Wiseguy

Bathroom Humor
by John Potty

How to Make Money
by B.A. Counterfeiter

Old Furniture
by Ann Teak

Learn to Dance
by N. Stepp

Timely Arrivals
by Justin Tyme

ED: Do you want this book on how to dig tunnels?
JED: No, it sounds boring.

What kind of vegetables do you always find in the library?
Quiet peas (please).

What would you get if you crossed a library with a golfer?

Book clubs.

What would you get if you crossed a library with insects that come out at night?

The Book of the Moth Club.

What do you need to be a good librarian?

Shelf control.

What did the librarian say when the duck rustled his feathers noisily?

"Quiet, down!"

HAIRDRESSER: What kind of hairstyle would you like?

LIBRARIAN: A page boy.

CARPENTER: I need a title that shows how to build a bookcase.
LIBRARIAN: Try the shelf help (self help) section.

WOMAN: Did Farmer Green come into the library today?
LIBRARIAN: Yes. He's in our weeding room.

Knock-Knock.
  Who's there?
Rhoda.
  Rhoda who?
Rhoda novel, but no one will read it.

WRITER: Just call me Ball Point.
EDITOR: Why?
WRITER: It's my pen name.

PRIEST: I'm looking for good books about Catholic Sisters.
LIBRARIAN: Try our nun-fiction section.

EDITOR: The King of England just wrote a book.
PUBLISHER: I guess he expects royalties.

What should you give a book when it's cold?
  A book jacket.

What is Santa's favorite novel about English knights?
  "Ivanhoe ho! ho!"

5.
ALPHA-BITS

What did the alphabet say after it fell down?
  I-M-O-K.

Which rock channel do the letters of the alphabet watch?
  M-T-V.

Where does Mr. Alphabet sit when he comes home from work?
  In his E-Z chair.

What does the alphabet wear on warm days?
  A T-shirt.

What monsters do you find in the haunted alphabet?

Killer B's.

Which letters make a great couple?

U-N-ME.

Which letters and number make a great cheer?

I-M-4-U!

Which letters and number can never go on a diet?

I-8-IT-ALL.

Which letters and what number tell you to be careful?

B-4-WARNED!

What kind of sale did the number store have?

2-4-1.

Which number and letters always get into trouble?

2-BAD.

Which letters in the alphabet are the smartest?

I-M.

MACK: What did the tired man say to the alphabet?
ZACK: Can I catch some Z's?

Which two letters mean you look nice?

Q-T.

Which letter of the alphabet do you find on roads and highways?

The U-Turn.

Which letter of the alphabet is never late?

B-on-time.

Which letter of the alphabet do you find near the ocean?

The C-Port.

What kind of soup does the alphabet like best?

P-Soup.

What would you get if you crossed a letter of the alphabet with a green vegetable?

T-peas.

Which letter and number when put together mean victory?

I-1.

6.
FUN FOOD

Why did the ghost go into the kitchen?
To scare up some food.

What did the termites have for dinner?
Table scraps.

What does a hungry garbage truck eat?
Junk food.

What would you get if you crossed gossip with soft margarine?
Rumors you can spread easily.

What would you get if you crossed a playground with ground ham?

Park sausage.

Why did the witch go into the kitchen?

To brew some coffee.

What monster makes loud noises while drinking soda?

The sea slurpant.

What food is made out of young reptiles who practice the martial arts?

Teenage Mutant Ninja Turtle Soup.

How do you make a werewolf breathe fire?

Feed him chili peppers.

DAFFYNITION
VEGETARIANS: People you don't have to meat.

FUN FOOD BOOKS

How to Prepare Meals
by I. Ken Cook

Tasty Recipes
by Etta Belle Food

Better Breakfasts
by Ronny Eggs

Fish for Supper
by Sam N. Stake

1,001 Sandwich Recipes
by Cole Supper

What did the beaver eat at the restaurant?
A tree course meal.

What vegetable do Alaskan sled dogs like?
Mushed potatoes.

MEL: Knock-Knock.
  NELL: Who's there?
MEL: Rice.
  NELL: Rice who?
MEL: Rice and shine.

CUSTOMER: I'd like a tasty dish.
WAITER: You're supposed to eat our food, sir, not
our dishes.

SILLY SLOGAN
ACME HOTDOG PACKAGERS—
We're not losers . . . we're wieners!

Why did the foxes move next door to a rabbit
family?
So they could have their neighbors over for dinner.

Why should you never invite a clock to dinner?
They always have seconds.

WAITER: Would you like to have a menu?
CUSTOMER: No, I'd rather have some food, please.

What did the lovesick lettuce say to the stove?
"You're baking my heart."

What did the head of lettuce take to school?
A looseleaf binder.

FLASH! Jack Frost likes cold cuts.

CEREAL: What do you want to do tonight?
MILK: Let's go bowling.

What did the scientist get when he crossed a
mattress with an oven?
   Breakfast in bed.

Supermarket manager to employees: Hey! When
the store closes, let's play checkers!

What diet guru lives in Transylvania?
   Count Calories.

Which Beatle song was about a deli treat?
Yellow Submarine Sandwich.

Knock-Knock.
Who's there?
Frosting.
Frosting who?
Frosting the morning, brush your teeth.

ED: Do bananas wear shoes?
FRED: No. They always wear slippers.

What do you get if you cross cooking fat with coconut trees?
Greased palms.

COOK: How can I think up new recipes for pasta?
WAITER: Use your noodle.

Why wouldn't the little watch's mother serve him dinner?

Because he didn't wash his hands.

What would you get if you crossed dinner with a watch?

Meal time.

SILLY SIGN

ACME CORN—

Let us box your ears.

Knock-Knock.
Who's there?
Venice.
Venice who?
Venice lunch?
I'm starved.

Knock-Knock.
Who's there?
Wilma.
Wilma who?
Wilma dinner be
ready soon?

Knock-Knock.
Who's there?
Barbie.
Barbie who?
Barbie-Q my steak.

What do sharks eat at barbecues?

Clamburgers.

43

7.
JUST KIDDING

Who tells nursery rhymes and is lumpy?
Mother Goose bumps.

Who lives in Mother Goose Land and is made of cabbage?
Old King Cole Slaw.

What monster lives in Mother Goose Land?
Little Bo Creep.

Why did Simple Simon take a trunk to the doctor's office?
He had a chest cold.

Who rides a tractor and makes great corned beef sandwiches?

The Farmer in the Deli.

When does Little Boy Blue blow his horn?

When he drives his car.

WACKY RUMOR: Humpty Dumpty is a great guy but he has scrambled eggs for brains!

MOTHER: Why did you spend all your allowance on candy?

BOY: Dad said to put my money where my mouth is.

CHIEF: What cable music channel do you get in your tent?

MEDICINE MAN: M-Teepee.

BOY: I flunked all of my courses. I flunked all of my courses.

MOM: Why did you say that twice?

BOY: Teacher told me I have to repeat this grade.

Why did the wristwatch get an "A" on the math test?

He knew his times tables.

BOY: Dad, I want to be a comedian.
FATHER: Don't make me laugh.

MATT: What do I get if I become an apprentice
knight?
SIR MORGAN: Three squire meals a day.

What did the boy say when he saw a buzzing insect
land on a clock?
Bee on time.

BOY: I can't believe I have all of this math
homework.
GIRL: Don't bother me. I have problems of my
own.

Why did the silly math student go to the bakery?
To find Pi.

**SIGN ON A PLAYGROUND EQUIPMENT
COMPANY**

COME TO OUR SLIDE SHOW.

Why did the squirrel gnaw through the side of the
house?
He was looking for wallnuts.

What size dress does a Queen Bee wear?
Size Hive.

46

What would you get if you crossed the Flintstones with a big stone in Ireland?
Fred and Blarney.

What would you get if you crossed cows with party games?
Moosical chairs.

What musical toy is the most athletic?
The Jock-in-the-Box.

SNOOPY: Did you see that new cartoon strip?
BROWNIE: No. I covered my eyes.

What does Tinkerbell drink from?
A pixie cup.

ED: What did the policeman say to the playground equipment?
NED: You can't park here.

LINNY: Did you buy duck feathers?
GINNY: Yes. They were marked down.

What would you get if you crossed a jogger with a four-leaf clover?
A run of good luck.

What chorus line performs at Prehistoric Radio City Music Hall?
The Bedrock-ettes.

CRAZY CHRISTMAS GREETINGS

From a Frog
Have a hoppy holiday season.

From the Internal Revenue Service
Many happy returns.

From a Honey Maker
Bee happy.

From a Spice Merchant
Season's greetings.

From a Breakfast Cereal Maker
Crispness Greetings.

From a Grower of Christmas Plants
Happy Holly Days.

From a Vegetable Farmer
Peas on earth.

Why did Santa Claus wear a cowboy hat and cowboy boots?

He was going to a western Ho-Ho-Hodown.

What would you get if you crossed Santa Claus with a flying saucer?

A U-F-HO!-HO!-HO!

Why didn't Scrooge mind getting coal for Christmas?

It helped him cut down on his heating bill.

What goes "bah! bah! bah! humbug"?

Ebeneezer Sheep.

What is Santa's favorite cowboy song?

"Ho-Ho-Home on the Range."

Who brings presents to skunks on Christmas?

Scent Nicholas.

What did Santa do at the barber shop?

Trimmed the Christmas trees.

8.
KNOCK-KNOCK!

Knock-Knock.
   Who's there?
Amen.
   Amen who?
Amen a bad mood!

Knock-Knock.
   Who's there?
Celery.
   Celery who?
Celery dance?

Knock-Knock.
   Who's there?
Distress.
   Distress who?
Distress matches my shoes.

Knock-Knock.
  Who's there?
Eileen.
  Eileen who?
Eileen over to tie my shoes.

Knock-Knock.
  Who's there?
Esau.
  Esau who?
Esau you coming and left.

Knock-Knock.
  Who's there?
Gwen.
  Gwen who?
Gwen you leave, close the door.

52

Knock-Knock.
Who's there?
Habit.
Habit who?
Habit your own way.

Knock-Knock.
Who's there?
Hairs.
Hairs who?
Hairs another fine mess you've gotten me into.

Knock-Knock.
Who's there?
Irish.
Irish who?
Irish I knew. I
have amnesia.

Knock-Knock.
Who's there?
I, Toad.
I, Toad who?
I, toad you I was
coming over!

Knock-Knock.
Who's there?
Jamaica.
Jamaica who?
Jamaica my lunch yet?

Knock-Knock.
Who's there?
Kennel.
Kennel who?
Kennel come out
if you ask him nicely.

Knock-Knock.
   Who's there?
Kenya.
   Kenya who?
Kenya come on out and play?

Knock-Knock.
   Who's there?
Less.
   Less who?
Less go shopping!

Knock-Knock.
   Who's there?
Luke.
   Luke who?
Luke out for falling rocks.

Knock-Knock.
   Who's there?
Menace.
   Menace who?
Menace the plural of "man."

Knock-Knock.
   Who's there?
Mist.
   Mist who?
Mist me! Nah!
Nah! Nah!

Knock-Knock.
   Who's there?
Rapper.
   Rapper who?
Rapper in a blanket.
She's cold.

Knock-Knock.
   Who's there?
Recited.
   Recited who?
Recited the enemy and we fired.

Knock-Knock.
  Who's there?
Retail.
  Retail who?
Retail stories around
the campfire.

Knock-Knock.
  Who's there?
Reveal.
  Reveal who?
Reveal sorry for you.

Knock-Knock.
  Who's there?
Sandy.
  Sandy who?
Sandy dirty clothes
to the cleaners.

Knock-Knock.
  Who's there?
Tillie.
  Tillie who?
Tillie apologizes
I won't forgive him.

Knock-Knock.
  Who's there?
Three chairs.
  Three chairs who?
Three chairs for the home team!

Knock-Knock.
  Who's there?
Urn.
  Urn who?
Urn your keep.

Knock-Knock.
  Who's there?
Vera.
  Vera who.
Vera you hiding?

Knock-Knock.
  Who's there?
Wanda.
  Wanda who?
Wanda where I put
the house key!

Knock-Knock!
  Who's there?
Wheat.
  Wheat who?
Wheat till the sun shines,
Nellie.

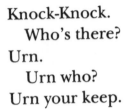

Knock-Knock.
  Who's there?
Wilder.
  Wilder who?
Wilder out let's raid the refrigerator.

Knock-Knock.
  Who's there?
Willie.
  Willie who?
Willie show up on time?

Knock-Knock.
  Who's there?
Wren.
  Wren who?
Wren in Rome do as the Romans do!

Knock-Knock.
  Who's there?
Yaw.
  Yaw who?
Way to cheer, cowboy!

Knock-Knock.
  Who's there?
Yawl.
  Yawl who?
Yawl be sorry.

Knock-Knock.
  Who's there?
Yukon.
  Yukon who?
Yukon open the door—it's safe.

9.
VET, PET AND WET

PET SHOP OWNER: You can't return that chimp.
MAN: Why not? Don't you have a monkey back
   guarantee?

What do sloppy cats leave behind after a picnic?
   Kitty litter.

ZACK: The hero of this jungle book is a lion.
MACK: How do you know that?
ZACK: He's the mane character.

VET: Where do you keep your sled dogs?
ALASKAN GUIDE: In a mush room.

What would you get if you crossed an oak with a St. Bernard?
A tree with a very loud bark.

Why did the dog go to court?
To pay a barking ticket.

VET: Your dog's nose isn't too hot.
BOY: His ears are ugly too, but I love him anyway.

Which Egyptian dog ruler died very young?
King Mutt.

What would you get if you crossed Lassie with a rose bush?

Collie-flowers.

What did the telephone operator say to the dog?

"You have a bone call."

What did the teacher say to the pig farmers?

"Don't talk until you raise your hams."

JOCKEY: Doc, is my sick horse all right?
VET: Yes. He's in stable condition.

What's woolly and floats in the ocean?

A cruise sheep (ship).

What do you say when a sheep sneezes?
"Bless ewe!"

Which sea creature is very sloppy?
The Loch Mess Monster.

ZACK: Which kind of fish swim alone?
MACK: Ones that haven't had any schooling.

What does a medieval farmer use to ride the waves?
A serf board.

What do sharks eat for dessert?
Fish cakes.

How do you catch an elephant fish?
Bait your hook with a peanut.

What has a rod, reel and a mane?
A fishing lion (line).

What kind of pet would you find in Fort Knox?
A gold fish.

ED: What kind of vehicle does Sergeant Goldfish drive?
JED: A fish tank.

WANT AD

Wanted: Cat to work with songbird act. Must be willing to keep mouth shut.

What do squid ride on?

An octobus.

What famous athlete swims underwater a lot?

Jock Cousteau.

What gymnastic stunt do fish like to perform?

Carp wheels (cartwheels).

What would you get if you crossed an octopus and a shark?

Something that's armed to the teeth.

What's soaking wet and wears a suit of armor?

A rainy knight.

What do you call a seasick ogre?

A green giant.

What did the vet say to the anxious buzzing insect?

"Bee patient."

10. THAT'S WHEELIE FUNNY!

What would you get if you crossed a comedian with a bicycle?

Someone who is wheel funny.

What would you get if you crossed turtles with automobiles?

Very slow traffic!

What do you find in a dinosaur junkyard?

T-Wrecks.

What has four wheels and goes "urp! urp! urp!"?
A hicc-up truck.

What do pigs use to carry their groceries?
Slopping carts.

Where does a car engine live?
In a motor home.

What's covered with red spots and drives cars into brick walls?
A rash dummy.

Why didn't the silly kid graduate from driving school?
She couldn't pass.

What has feathers and operates an 18-wheeler?
A cluck driver.

What kind of shoes with wheels do penguins wear?
Polar skates.

What does Mother Air Rifle use to take her infant for a walk?
A B-B carriage.

SALESMAN: Would you like to buy a car battery?
CUSTOMER: Only if you'll charge it.

What is the automobile's favorite TV game show?
"Wheel of Fortune."

What has wheels and goes "slosh! slosh!"?
A car pool.

What kind of car did the elephant want?
One with lots of trunk space.

What would you get if you crossed an automobile with a pot of glue?
A car with a sticky shift.

What happens when boy tire meets girl tire?
They go around together.

What has wheels and plays the Frankenstein monster in old movies?
Boris Car-loff.

What kind of transportation do ballerinas take?
Tutu trains.

LOCOMOTIVE (*to boxcar*): Watch it pal, I've got a lot of pull around here.

Why did the locomotive feel so important?
It was a track star.

CONDUCTOR: Why are you insulting that old locomotive?
ENGINEER: Because it works best when it's all steamed up.

What locomotives do you see in fashion magazines?
Model trains.

SILLY SLOGANS

ACME ROAD MAP PUBLISHERS—We know where we're going.

ACME STEERING WHEEL COMPANY—Let us turn things around for you.

ACME BIRD CANDY—A sweet tweet for your pet!

What has lots of wheels and looks like a big bee?
A Greyhound buzz.

How do you drive a cattle car?
Steer it.

What has a powder puff and four wheels?
A compact car.

What honks a lot and has wheels?
A flock of geese on a bus.

What has two wheels and laughs a lot?
A ha-ha-Harley-Davidson motorcycle.

What insect has four wheels and lives at the beach?
The dune buggy.

CAR: Why is that baby tire crying?
AUTO: It needs to be changed.

Why couldn't the tire buy anything?
It was flat broke.

What do you put on toasted cars?
Traffic jam.

Why did the sheep driver tie up traffic?
He kept making ewe turns.

ZACK: That car has claws on its hood.
MACK: It's probably a taxi crab.

Why did the car have an upset stomach?
It had too much gas.

What famous car lives in a church tower?
The Hatchback of Notre Dame.

How did the car pass its demolition derby test?
It took a crash course.

ZACK: That locomotive isn't too smart.
MACK: That's because it has a one-track mind.

Where do big trucks go to have fun?
To a trailer park.

What do you call an antelope who sells cars?
A gnu car dealer.

What would you get if you crossed an automobile
with a kangaroo?
A car that's easy to jump start.

What must a car have to be a great athlete?
Good motor skills.

Where should you take a damaged car?
To a bruised car lot.

What has four wheels, pulls cars, and goes "ouch!
ouch!"?
A sore toe truck.

Knock-Knock.
Who's there?
Wheel.
Wheel who?
Wheel see you later.

Why did the stupid driver let his car crash?
He didn't want to brake it.

Why did the new car talk so much?
It came equipped with a hot air bag.

What do tires wear to keep warm?
Hub caps.

Why did the police cars go to the automobile junkyard?
To look for car hoods.

What should you do with a wet tire?
Spin dry it.

AL: How did you know your car was in pain?
HAL: Its brakes kept screeching.

What did the car say to the gas pump?
"You can't fuel me!"

What do you get if you cross an executioner and a plane with no motor?
A hang glider.

70

What do you get if you cross a jet and a motorcycle?

A sonic vroom.

What holds eight passengers and is totally out of sight?

The Invisible Van.

Show me a motorist who has a fender bender with a police car . . . and I'll show you a driver who's had a run-in with the law.

MAN: How much do these old batteries cost?
CLERK: Nothing. They're free of charge.

What does the girlfriend of Mickey Mouse drive?

A minnie van.

11.
WORKING FOR THE FUN OF IT

Why did the sorceress go to the beauty school?
To learn to wave her wand.

MARY: I make pressed flowers for a living.
LARRY: Is it fun?
MARY: No. It's cut and dried.

EMPLOYEE: Boss, my mind is shot.
BOSS: Oh, yeah? Well, I do the firing around here.

What would you get if you crossed a thundercloud with a bankbook?

Rain checks.

What would you get if you crossed a bankbook with a math teacher?

Money problems.

What would you get if you crossed a gardener and a fortune teller?

Someone who weeds palms.

ZACK: How's your exterminator business?
MACK: I'm still working out the bugs.

TED: Do you like being a watch repairman?
ED: It has its moments.

SON: I want to be a minister.
DAD: Heaven help you!

NUTTY NOTE

Playwrights put words in other people's mouths.

AEROBICS TEACHER: My business is slow.
FITNESS INSTRUCTOR: Things will work out.

Why did the boxer sign up for gymnastics class?

He wanted to learn how to roll with the punches.

THE DIZZY DOCTOR

"Doctor, doctor, my wife thinks she's an acrobat."

"I'll stop her from flipping out."

"Doctor, doctor, my husband thinks he's a car."

"Don't let him drive you crazy."

"Doctor, doctor, my son thinks he's an ant."

"He's just trying to bug you."

"Doctor, doctor, my daughter thinks she's a sheet of music."

"Bring her in and I'll take some notes."

"Doctor, doctor, I keep thinking about rubber bands."

"Well, snap out of it!"

"Doctor, doctor, you've got to help me. I think I'm a kangaroo."

"Quick, hop up on my couch!"

"Doctor, doctor, I'm sick as a dog!"

"I know a good vet I can send you to."

BONE DOCTOR: Business is really bad.
NURSE: What you need is a lucky break.

Why did the math teacher go to a psychologist?
He needed help with his problems.

What do you call a person who pushes a broom
and snores?
A sweepwalker.

What marshall works for the Internal Revenue
Service?
A Taxes Ranger.

LAW STUDENT #1: Let's pretend we're in court.
LAW STUDENT #2: I'm not in the moot.

EDITOR: Why do you print your books on fly
    paper?
PUBLISHER: So people can't put them down.

What do lady roller skaters wear to fancy parties?
High-wheeled shoes.

Show me a math teacher who becomes a minister . . . and I'll show you a guy who counts his blessings.

Show me a king with a sore throat . . . and I'll show you a guy with a royal pain in the neck.

MR. SMITH: Why aren't you president of the mortgage company anymore?
MR. JONES: Frankly, I lost interest.

CRAZY COMPANY SLOGANS

ACME WOODEN DOORS
Go Ahead! Knock Our Product

ACME LAWN SERVICE SCHOOL
We'll Show You How to Make Mow Money

ACME JUMP ROPE SCHOOL
Skip Class

ACME LEATHER COMPANY
We Have Lots to Hide

ACME SPEEDY COMMUNICATIONS
Let Us Give You the Fax

ACME VIDEO GAME COMPANY
We're in Business for the Fun of It

THE V MOTOR COMPANY
We're Right Behind U

ANDY: What does a witch teacher use to correct
    spelling tests?
RANDY: A magic marker.

What does a Transylvanian dentist use to pull out
fangs?
  Vampliers.

SIGNING OFF

SIGN ON A WINDOW SHADE
COMPANY

LOVE IS NOT ALWAYS BLINDS.

SIGN ON AN AIR-CONDITIONED
BANQUET HALL

WE ALWAYS GIVE YOU A COOL RECEPTION.

SIGN ON A MUSIC SCHOOL

**STUDENTS ARE ALLOWED TO PLAY DURING
CLASS.**

SIGN IN A SHOELACE TESTING PLANT

KNOT DURING WORKING HOURS.

How do you fire a lady who works in a lingerie
department?

Give her a pink slip.

FUNNY FACT
Never date barbers.
They give everyone the brush-off.

What did the policeman say to the lumberjack?

"Chop in the name of the law."

UNION DUES

THE BASEBALL UMPIRES' UNION
We decide when to call strikes.

THE BASKETBALL REFS' UNION
Experts in foul play.

THE FENCE INSTALLERS' UNION
We have great picket lines.

THE HOUSEKEEPERS' UNION
Don't mess with us.

THE DOUGHNUT MAKERS' UNION
Bake us an offer.

THE AIRPLANE PILOTS' UNION
We demand high pay.

WHAT KIND OF MUSIC DO YOU LIKE?

"Heavy metal," said the iron worker.

"Hard rock," said the geologist.

"Blue grass," said the gardener.

"Swing," said the playground equipment manufacturer.

"Pop music," said the father-to-be.

Why did the coach send a monster into the football game?

Because his team needed a field ghoul.

HOW'S BUSINESS?

ACME TOUPEE COMPANY
Business has been falling off.

ACME STEAK COMPANY
Things are tough.

ACME CLOCK COMPANY
Times are bad.

ACME FURNACE COMPANY
We're in hot water.

Show me a man who's putting a roof over a clock tower . . . and I'll show you a man who's working overtime.

What does King Kong use to fix a leaky pipe?
A monkey wrench.

What football player drinks a lot of lemon juice?
The bitter end.

12.
CHUCKLE CHILLERS

What's scary and carries swords?
   The Three Boo-sketeers.

What do you get if you cross Dr. Jekyll with a playground?
   Dr. Jekyll and Mr. Slide.

What game does Dr. Jekyll love to play?
   Hyde and Go Seek.

SANDI: I'm in love with the Invisible Man.
MANDI: What do you see in him?

MAD SCIENTIST: I crossed a witch doctor with
    morning mist.
GHOUL: What did you get?
MAD SCIENTIST: Voodew.

What did everyone say when the witch walked
down the aisle?
   "Here comes the bride and broom."

What does a witch wear on her wrist?
   A charm bracelet.

What did the witch say after she buried her
treasure?
   "Hex marks the spot!"

83

Why did the witch go to the hospital?
She needed some hex-rays.

What do witches sell at flea markets?
Witch crafts.

CREEP: Does Dracula play tennis?
GHOUL: No, but he loves bat-minton.

How did Dracula break his fangs?
Learning you can't get blood from a stone.

PERSONAL
Dracula wants to meet girl with appetite for
adventure. *Object:* To go out for a bite.

Why did Dracula climb up on the barn roof?
To get to the weather vein.

Why would Dracula make a good policeman?
He'd take a bite out of crime.

Why did Dracula run away from the Gold Rush?
A prospector wanted to stake Drac to a claim.

What does Dracula use to make vampire pancakes?
Bat-ter.

Knock-Knock.
　Who's there?
Eben.
　Eben who?
Eben bitten by a vampire.

Which dinosaur is Dracula afraid of?
The Stakeasaurus.

DRACULA:　I just bit a dwarf on the neck.
VAMPIRE:　Oh, Drac! How could you stoop so low!

ZACK:　Does Dr. Frankenstein like to do aerobics?
MACK:　Nah. He's a body builder.

What do you call a cowboy who jumps on the
Frankenstein Monster's back and yells "Giddyup"?
A cowpoke who rides the strange.

WHY DID FRANKENSTEIN GO TO A PSYCHIATRIST?

. . . He thought he had a screw loose.

. . . He felt like he was coming apart at the seams.

. . . He couldn't pull himself together.

What is the Frankenstein monster's favorite therapy?
Shock treatments.

IVAN: Dracula refused to run a race against Frankenstein.
IGOR: Why did he do that?
IVAN: Because he thought the competition was too stiff.

MRS. WOLF: There's a ghoul in your kitchen.
MRS. FRANKENSTEIN: Relax. That's just our housecreeper.

What has fangs and flies?
A werewolf on a hang glider.

Why did the werewolf hold his hand up to his ear?
Because he always listened to his paw.

ZACK: Why did the mad doctor go to the cemetery?

MACK: To treat a grave illness.

What did the mad doctor say to Igor while he was building his monster?

"Hey, Igor, come here and give me a hand."

Which famous ape writes best-selling horror novels?

Stephen King Kong.

What do you call an author who keeps turning out books after he dies?

A ghost writer.

What monster lives in a nice house in the Italian countryside?

Godvilla.

Why did Godzilla eat the ships in Hong Kong Harbor?

He loved junk food.

NAT: Godzilla's in New York!

PAT: I guess he's polishing off the Big Apple.

What giant monster has a pea brain?

Podzilla.

Which giant monster is really clumsy?

Clodzilla.

What city devoured by Godzilla refused to stay down?

Tokyo-yo.

PERSONAL

Godzilla wants to meet giant lady monster.
Object: To step out on the town.

What would you get if you crossed Godzilla with Merlin's magic wand?
A lizard wizard.

What does Godzilla have on the walls of his bathroom?
Rep-tiles.

IGOR: Why did the Children of the Corn get lost?
IVAN: They couldn't find their way out of the maize.

Knock-Knock.
  Who's there?
Eerie.
  Eerie who?
Eerie is! Grab him before he escapes!

Knock-Knock
  Who's there?
I, Spectre.
  I, Spectre, who?
I, spectre to scream any minute!

What monster goes "caw! caw!" and lives in the Himalayan Mountains?
The Abominable Crowman.

What does the Abominable Snowman put his ice cream in?
A snowcone.

Where did Cinderella Yeti go?
To the snow ball.

Knock-Knock.
   Who's there?
Icy.
   Icy who?
Icy you, but you can't see me.

What would you get if you crossed a yeti with a turtle?

The Abominable Slowman.

What does the Abominable Snowman have for breakfast?

Frosted Flakes.

What does the Abominable Snowman eat at a ballgame?

A chilly (chili) dog.

What does the Abominable Snowman eat on Thanksgiving Day?

Cold turkey.

What does the Abominable Snowman eat for dessert?

Frozen custard.

What did the health-conscious Abominable Snowman eat at snack time?

Frozen yogurt.

What does the Abominable Snowman use in his coffee?

Cold cream.

FRIGHTFUL FLASH! The Mummy loves rap music!

THE SNOWMAN'S SHOPPING LIST

Cold cuts.

Iced tea.

Frozen yogurt.

Frosted Flakes Cereal.

BIZARRE BOOKS

My Life as a Werewolf—by Harry Beast

I Don't Want to Be a Zombie—by Barry McQuick

The Homeless Vampire—by Anita Coffin

Godzilla's Cookbook—by I. Etta City

The Invisible Man Disappears—by I.M. Gone

My House Is Haunted—by I. Shaw Ghosts

WEIRD WORDS OF WISDOM

ON THE TOMB OF A MEMORY EXPERT . . .
Gone but Not Forgotten.

ON THE TOMB OF A CUSTODIAN . . .
Sweep in Peace.

ON THE TOMB OF A COMEDIAN . . .
Jest in Peace.

ON THE TOMB OF A HOUSEKEEPER . . .
Duster to Dust!

ON THE TOMB OF A SHORT-ORDER COOK . . .
Hashes to Ashes.

Show me Big Foot running a marathon . . . and I'll show you some of the world's biggest race tracks!

Why did Mr. Skeleton wear a hat on the middle of his leg?
It was a knee cap.

FLASH! The Abominable Snowman drinks freeze-dried coffee.

What do police ghosts wear under their coats?
Boo-let-proof vests.

What's ugly, wears feathers and dances in a chorus line in Las Vegas?
Show Ghouls.

Which two letters of the alphabet say good-bye?
C-U.

INDEX